Author:

Thomas Ratliff studied American History at Central Connecticut State University and the University of Connecticut. He has taught English and history in junior and senior schools, as well as history and secondary education courses at college level. He is also co-author of several young adult historical novels set in the Civil War era.

Artist:

David Antram was born in Brighton, England, in 1958. He studied at Eastbourne College of Art and then worked in advertising for fifteen years before becoming a full-time artist. He has illustrated many children's non-fiction books.

Series creator:

David Salariya was born in Dundee, Scotland. He has illustrated a wide range of books and has created and designed many new series for publishers both in the UK and overseas. In 1989, he established The Salariya Book Company. He lives in Brighton with his wife, illustrator Shirley Willis, and their son Jonathan.

Editor:

Karen Barker Smith

Assistant Editor:

Michael Ford

Schools Library & Museum Service
Unit D
Ropemaker Park
HAILSHAM
East Sussex BN27 3GU
Tel: 01323 466380

Published in Great Britain in 2004 by
Book House, an imprint of
The Salariya Book Company Ltd
25 Marlborough Place, Brighton BN1 1UB

S A L A R I Y A

HB ISBN-13: 978-1-904194-95-8
PB ISBN-13: 978-1-904194-96-5

Please visit the Salariya Book Company at:
www.salariya.com
www.book-house.co.uk

A catalogue record
for this book is available
from the British Library.

Printed and bound in China.

Printed on paper
from sustainable forests.

Reprinted in 2008.

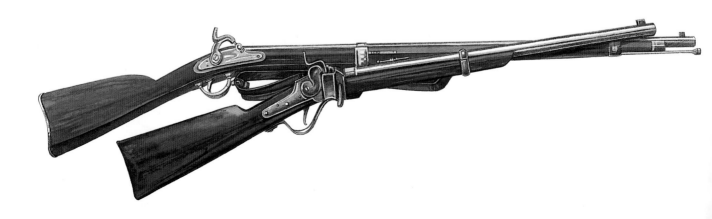

Avoid being a US Civil War Soldier!

Written by
Thomas Ratliff

Illustrated by
David Antram

Created and designed by
David Salariya

The Danger Zone

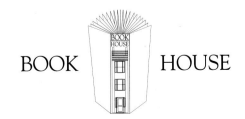

BOOK HOUSE

Contents

Introduction

You are a farmer living in a small town in Connecticut, in the United States of America. After the election of Abraham Lincoln as president of the country in 1860, eleven southern states worried about the issue of slavery decide to secede – to leave the United States and form their own country, the Confederate States of America. Within a few months war breaks out. In the North people want to preserve the Union and get the seceded states to return; in the South most people want to preserve slavery and keep their new independence.

In the spring of 1861 President Lincoln calls for volunteers to sign up for 90-day enlistments in the army. You decide to serve your country and join the Union Army. Everyone expects the war to be over in a few months, but in fact you will remain in the army for the next four years. In that time, over two million men will serve in the Union Army, compared to about 700,000 for the Confederates. Casualties for both sides will total 620,000 deaths, making the conflict America's bloodiest war.

Hurrah for the regiment!

You have enlisted in one of your state's infantry regiments. This means you will be serving with people from your home town and surrounding communities. The regiment has about 1,000 soldiers, divided into ten companies. You are one of 82 privates in Company K under Sergeant Wilson.

Your regiment is part of the Army of the Potomac, stationed just outside Washington, DC, the capital of the USA. The army is supposed to protect Washington and threaten the Confederate capital at Richmond, Virginia, 160 km to the south. Opposing you is the Army of Northern Virginia, commanded by General Robert E. Lee. Throughout the war these two large armies will fight many terrible battles.

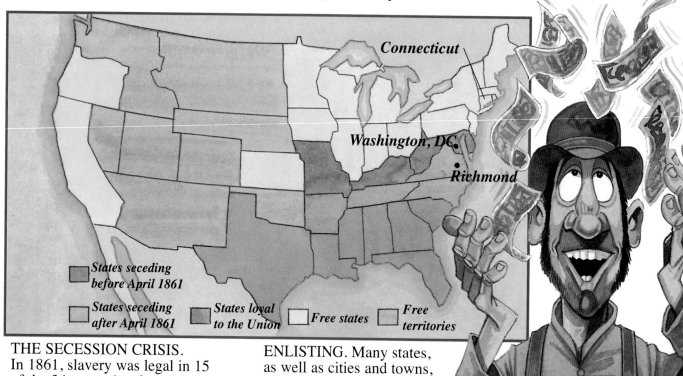

Connecticut

Washington, DC

Richmond

- States seceding before April 1861
- States seceding after April 1861
- States loyal to the Union
- Free states
- Free territories

THE SECESSION CRISIS. In 1861, slavery was legal in 15 of the 34 states, but four slave states, Delaware, Maryland, Kentucky and Missouri did not secede. West Virginia, originally a part of Virginia, became a state in 1863.

ENLISTING. Many states, as well as cities and towns, offered bonuses for enlisting in the army. The bonuses could add up to several hundred dollars (far more than a year's basic soldier pay).

Union cavalry soldier

If you are married, bring your wife along. Although most wives stayed at home, some women followed their husbands during the war. Married women often cooked meals, mended and washed clothes and tended to the sick and wounded.

It'll be just like home – cooking, mending, washing – you'll love it Mildred.

You varmint! I tell you, I don't want to go!

Union artillery soldier

Union infantry soldier

INFANTRY, ARTILLERY AND CAVALRY. There are three kinds of military units: infantry, or foot soldiers; cavalry, who rode horses; and artillery, soldiers assigned to fire cannons. Like you, most soldiers in the Civil War fought in the infantry.

Cannonballs

What's life like in the Union Army?

Who's who?

You can tell from the brass insignia on a soldier's cap whether they are in the infantry, cavalry, or artillery. Your cap has a bugle, which signifies the infantry.

Cavalry cap

Infantry cap

Artillery cap

Life in the army is very different from how it was on your farm. Everything you do is governed by regulations. All soldiers have to wear Union Army uniforms, which are blue with brass buttons. You have a wool cap with a leather brim. The uniforms are wool, which keep you warm in winter, but they are hot and itchy in the summer. Food in the army is not as good as you are used to. Each week your company gets supplies – pork or salted beef, flour or hard bread (called 'hardtack'), beans, peas, coffee, sugar and salt – to feed all the men. Your company has a cook to prepare the meals, but regulations state that he has to boil the meat and vegetables for several hours, so the food is not very tasty.

Company cook

I'm boiling it for another three hours – it's company rules.

WATER. During battle you will get very thirsty. You can't just get up in the middle of a fight and go to look for water. Keep your canteen with you at all times!

Water canteen

Handy hint

Even if you don't like the food, eat when you can. On a long march or in battle, the only food you can carry is hardtack, which makes your mouth very dry.

How about YOU do the washing and my WIFE does the cooking?

SALARY. A private in the Union Army earns $12 a month. In the 1860s you can eat in a restaurant for 25 cents, mail a letter for three cents and buy a suit of clothes for about $2. Most soldiers had some of their pay sent home to their families.

Will I have my own toilet and bedroom?

Bedroll

Pack

Rifle

Canteen

Unfortunately you will be spending most of the time outdoors. You share a small, two-man tent which is really two halves that button together. When you are marching, the tent is taken apart – you carry half the tent and your tent-mate carries the other. But if you are marching long distances or engaged in battle, you won't have the time to set up your tent and will often just sleep on the ground. During the winter, there isn't much fighting. Many soldiers in your company build huts to live in and collect furniture to make life more comfortable. Some even have small stoves to keep warm. But in the spring, when the fighting starts up again, you have to throw out everything you cannot carry with you.

FULLY DRESSED. A soldier carries all of his gear in a pack, including clothes, dishes and silverware, personal items and a bedroll. You also carry your canteen, rifle, bayonet and cartridge box.

Summer

Winter

KEEPING CLEAN. If you want to take a bath, you will have to find a pond or river, which might be fun in the summertime, but is almost impossible in the winter. On marches or during battle, you won't have time to wash, comb your hair, brush your teeth, or change your clothes.

10

On long marches you can have some of your gear, like your tent and extra ammunition, carried in wagons. Since you may have to march several kilometres a day, the lighter your pack the better.

Handy hint

That looks heavy.

Snore! snort ... groan....

SPARE TIME. You and your friends will have lots of time on your hands in the winter. To amuse themselves, the men in your company like to play baseball or dice, organise singing and storytelling groups, or write letters home. Post from home is important as it keeps up morale.

The first battle

A few kilometres south of Washington is Manassas, Virginia – an important railway junction and a key location for moving men and supplies. Union generals decide to capture the railway and your unit is part of a large force that marches south toward Manassas. Confederate forces move north from Richmond and a battle is imminent. The fighting starts early in the morning. Deployed along a small creek called Bull Run, you don't really see the enemy, although you fire your weapon a few times when ordered to do so. The battle is mostly loud noises and smoke and it is hard to tell who is winning. About 4 pm the Confederates receive reinforcements and you are ordered to retreat. The first battle has ended in defeat! You are hot, tired and very thirsty, but you have to march all the way back to Washington before you can rest.

SPECTATORS. Many people from Washington came to observe the battle. They were dressed in their best clothes and some brought picnic lunches. The road to Washington was clogged that evening by thousands of retreating soldiers and wagons filled with frightened civilians.

Another glass of champers Dolly?

Was life different for a Confederate soldier?

In the Confederate Army, cavalry soldiers (right) have to supply their own horses. You have to be a very good horseman to ride in the cavalry.

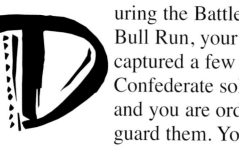
I hope you boys like hardtack and beans.

During the Battle of Bull Run, your unit captured a few Confederate soldiers and you are ordered to guard them. You learn that the life of a Confederate soldier is not so different to your own. Their uniforms are grey wool, similar to yours, but not all Confederates have uniforms and some don't even have shoes! They have muskets instead of rifles, but many are excellent soldiers and the Confederate generals are experienced and skilled. The food in the Confederate Army is not as good, or as plentiful, as you are used to and they have fewer doctors and nurses. But they are Americans, just like you. You realise that the Southern soldiers have to endure the same hardships you do: living outdoors, long marches in extreme heat or cold, loneliness and homesickness and the dangers of battle. Throughout the war, soldiers from each side will often treat each other like friends and trade news, stories and even goods like coffee and tobacco.

Confederate cavalry soldier

Handy hint

Try not to get captured! Even if prisoners of war are treated well, many still die of malnutrition, disease, or from a lack of clean drinking water.

What, no grits?

DIFFERENT BACKGROUNDS. Most Confederate soldiers grew up on farms and are used to horses and guns. Southerners expect their soldiers to be superior to Northern soldiers, many of whom are from cities and have never fired a gun before.

The seesaw battles of 1862

n the spring of 1862, your unit goes into action again, this time on the peninsula east of Richmond. In a series of battles known as the Seven Days, the Union Army is forced to retreat to Washington. A few months later, General Lee launches an invasion of the North. Your unit marches for several days in a row to catch up with the Confederates and the two armies meet at the town of Sharpsburg, Maryland. Union troops, deployed along Antietam Creek, see plenty of action. The fighting is terrible and it seems that neither side is going to win. But by nightfall, you see that the Confederates are retreating. Your entire regiment lets out a loud cheer. Your first victory!

Victory at Antietam

That'll show 'em!

A BLOODY DAY. The joy of victory does not last long as you are assigned to help collect the dead and wounded (below). The Battle of Antietam – also known as the Battle of Sharpsburg – was the worst day of fighting in the war so far, with over 12,000 casualties on both sides.

FREEDOM. After Antietam, President Lincoln issues the Emancipation Proclamation, which frees all the slaves in the Confederacy. During the war, over 179,000 African-Americans serve in the Union Army.

Handy hint

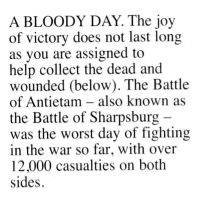

It is always better to defend a position than to attack. One reason for the high number of casualties at Antietam is that both sides were attacking in the open, with no defensive protection.

President Abraham Lincoln

...I do order and declare that all persons held as slaves henceforward shall be free...

I need a holiday.

The aftermath of Antietam

17

What kind of weapons will I use?

Union cavalry sword

Many Union weapons are made in your home state of Connecticut. Sharps rifles are popular as they can be loaded and fired faster than the older muskets. Colt Firearms produce revolvers which fire six shots without reloading. These are popular with cavalrymen, as it is difficult to reload while riding. You are proud to carry a modern Sharps rifle. Many Southern soldiers still use more inaccurate muskets. To load a musket the gunpowder and a lead ball are put into the muzzle and then a small amount of powder is put in the priming pan. When the trigger is pulled, the hammer strikes the priming pan and gives off a small spark, igniting the powder and firing the musket. A trained soldier can load and fire his musket up to three times a minute.

CAVALRY SOLDIERS are equipped with swords and pistols. The sword comes in handy when there is hand-to-hand fighting.

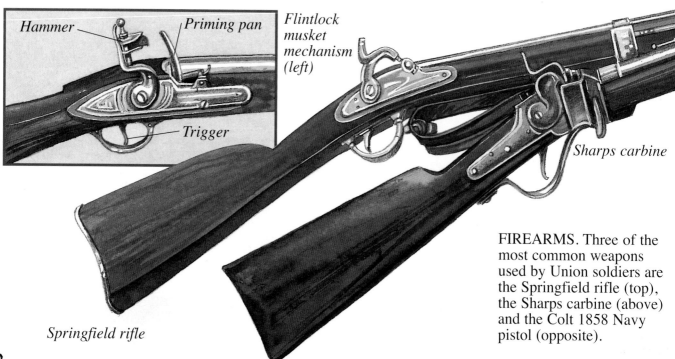

Hammer

Priming pan

Flintlock musket mechanism (left)

Trigger

Sharps carbine

Springfield rifle

FIREARMS. Three of the most common weapons used by Union soldiers are the Springfield rifle (top), the Sharps carbine (above) and the Colt 1858 Navy pistol (opposite).

Charge!

Handy hint

Your cartridge box holds about 40 cartridges for your Sharps rifle. Keep track of how many you fire. If you run out you might not be able to find more straight away.

Colt Navy pistol

Thud!

Whack

Gulp!

Grind!

AN AMAZING VICTORY.
At Gettysburg, a Union unit from Maine ran out of ammunition while defending a position. However, they still managed to defeat an attacking Confederate regiment by charging into them and overwhelming the attackers in hand-to-hand combat.

19

Turning points: Gettysburg and Vicksburg

PROBLEMS ON THE MARCH. Marching in the summer is unpleasant. It is hot, thirsty work and the dust is unbearable. To make matters worse, your wool uniform is so itchy you can hardly stand it.

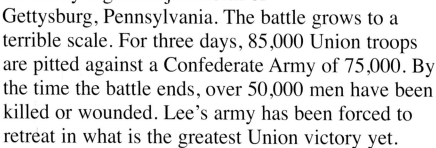

I n June 1863, Lee launches an invasion into Pennsylvania. The Army of the Potomac, now commanded by General Meade, moves quickly to intercept the Confederates. On 1st July your unit runs into an enemy regiment just north of Gettysburg, Pennsylvania. The battle grows to a terrible scale. For three days, 85,000 Union troops are pitted against a Confederate Army of 75,000. By the time the battle ends, over 50,000 men have been killed or wounded. Lee's army has been forced to retreat in what is the greatest Union victory yet.

General Robert E. Lee

General George Gordon Meade

On the same day Confederate forces in Vicksburg, Mississippi, surrender the city to a Union army under General Ulysses S. Grant. Grant had laid siege to the city for several months and the surrender meant that the Union army controlled the Mississippi River. Five months after these battles, a national cemetery was dedicated at Gettysburg by President Lincoln.

Handy hint

If you are wounded you might find help from civilians who live nearby. Many of the homes in Gettysburg were turned into hospitals after the battle.

What if I'm wounded?

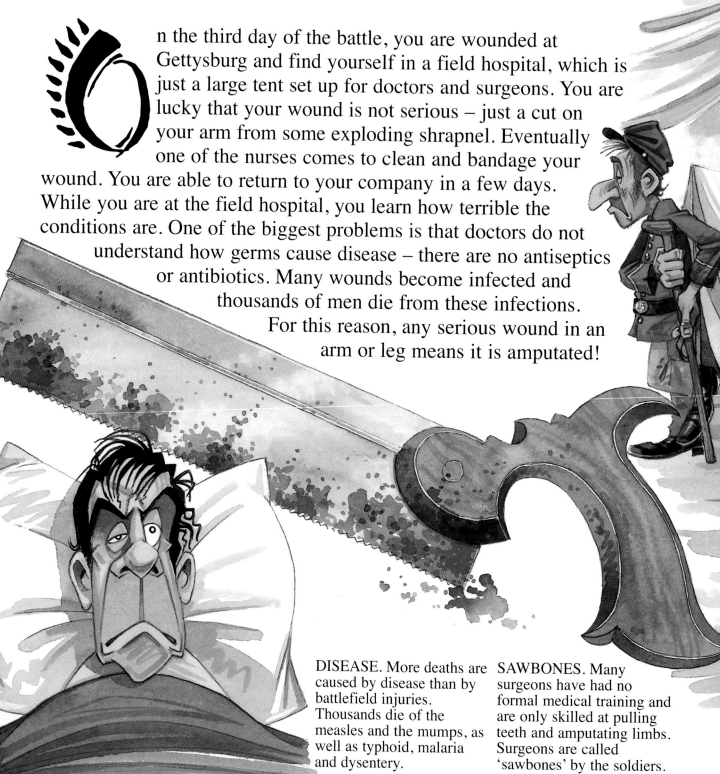

O n the third day of the battle, you are wounded at Gettysburg and find yourself in a field hospital, which is just a large tent set up for doctors and surgeons. You are lucky that your wound is not serious – just a cut on your arm from some exploding shrapnel. Eventually one of the nurses comes to clean and bandage your wound. You are able to return to your company in a few days. While you are at the field hospital, you learn how terrible the conditions are. One of the biggest problems is that doctors do not understand how germs cause disease – there are no antiseptics or antibiotics. Many wounds become infected and thousands of men die from these infections. For this reason, any serious wound in an arm or leg means it is amputated!

DISEASE. More deaths are caused by disease than by battlefield injuries. Thousands die of the measles and the mumps, as well as typhoid, malaria and dysentery.

SAWBONES. Many surgeons have had no formal medical training and are only skilled at pulling teeth and amputating limbs. Surgeons are called 'sawbones' by the soldiers.

What about the navy?

FIGHTING IN THE NAVY.
All sailors are issued with weapons and trained in their use, but there is very little hand-to-hand fighting between ships' crews in battle.

When you have time you write to your cousin who enlisted in the Union Navy. According to him the Union Navy had 42 ships at the beginning of the war. One of the Navy's strategies was to blockade all Southern ports, but to control the enormous coastline the number of ships had to be increased. By the end of the war there are 671 fighting ships and the US Navy is the largest in the world.

thud

" ...lucky to be on a ship, as we don't have to march everywhere like you do and I think that the food we get is probably better than what you describe... "

24

In one letter, your cousin describes the most famous naval battle of the war. Most ships in the 1860s were made of wood, but the Union *Monitor* and the Confederate *Merrimack* (also known as the C.S.S. *Virginia*) were different – they were ironclads. In March 1862 the two ships engaged in a three-hour battle. Each took at least two dozen direct hits, but the cannonballs bounced off the iron plating and neither ship sustained serious damage. The battle ended because the crews were so exhausted they could not load the cannons any more.

Handy hint

It is much safer in the navy. Of the 100,000 men who serve in the Union Navy, only about 200 are killed and less than 200 are wounded.

"...the smoke was so thick at times that you couldn't see the ships at all. It was exciting to watch but frightening to think about future sea battles..."

25

1864 – Total war

In early 1864, General Grant is appointed commander of the Army of the Potomac. In May, he begins a series of battles against Lee that slowly pushes the Confederate Army backwards to Richmond and then beyond to the railway centre of Petersburg, Virginia. For several weeks, your unit is marching, fighting and marching again. You don't get any time to rest or write letters and many nights you don't get any sleep at all. Some of the fighting is the worst you have experienced in the war. At Petersburg, the Confederates dig trenches and set up strong earthworks which are too well-defended to attack. For the next few months your unit is camped outside Petersburg. The war is a stalemate, with the Union Army slowly starving out the Confederates in a siege.

ULYSSES S. GRANT. Grant (left) becomes the most successful Union general. When the war started, he was working in his brother's store in Ohio – by the end of the war he is one of the most famous generals of all time. Grant becomes so popular that he is elected president in 1868 and 1872.

How does it all end?

THE END OF THE LINE. In his retreat, Lee was trying to join forces with another Confederate Army in North Carolina. When he realised he was surrounded, he was forced to surrender.

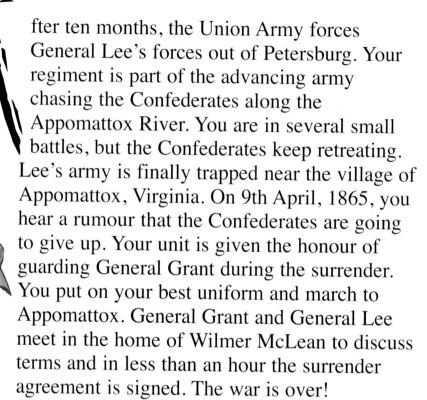

After ten months, the Union Army forces General Lee's forces out of Petersburg. Your regiment is part of the advancing army chasing the Confederates along the Appomattox River. You are in several small battles, but the Confederates keep retreating. Lee's army is finally trapped near the village of Appomattox, Virginia. On 9th April, 1865, you hear a rumour that the Confederates are going to give up. Your unit is given the honour of guarding General Grant during the surrender. You put on your best uniform and march to Appomattox. General Grant and General Lee meet in the home of Wilmer McLean to discuss terms and in less than an hour the surrender agreement is signed. The war is over!

In 1861, Wilmer McLean was living near Manassas, Virginia. His house was used by Confederate generals as a command post during the first battle. Some people say the war began and ended in Mr McLean's living room.

THE WAR IS OVER! In American cities church bells ring out in celebration. After four years of fighting, you can finally go home to your family farm in Connecticut.

If you are a Confederate soldier, you can keep your guns, horses and mules. Most men in the South were farmers and General Grant allowed them to leave with the things that would be useful when they returned to normal lives.

Handy hint

I'll be huntin' with this!

It looks much better on you.

29

Glossary

Amputation Having a part of your body, particularly a limb, cut off by a surgeon.

Artillery Units of soldiers that transport and fire cannons in battle.

Blockade To prevent ships from entering or leaving a port.

Canteen A water bottle.

Carbine A lightweight rifle with a short barrel.

Cartridge box A leather box that holds ammunition for a rifle.

Casualty A person who is wounded, missing, killed, or captured in battle.

Cavalry Soldiers who fight on horseback.

Company A military unit of about 100 men. Ten companies make a regiment.

Deployed Positioned, as in a battle or for defensive purposes.

Earthworks Walls of earth and logs which soldiers build for protection.

Enlist To join the army.

Field hospital A temporary hospital set up near a battle to care for the wounded.

Grits Broken grains of corn that are used in many recipes in the southern United States.

Hardtack A hard biscuit or bread made with only flour and water.

Infantry Soldiers who fight on foot.

Insignia A badge of office, rank, or membership.

Ironclad A ship with iron plating on the outside.

Malnutrition Not having enough good food to maintain one's health.

Morale The general level of confidence and happiness.

Musket A long-barrelled muzzle-loading gun used by the Confederate infantry.

Private The lowest ranking enlisted soldier in the army.

Regiment A military unit of about 1,000 men.

Reinforcements Additional soldiers who are added to help in a battle.

Secede To leave an organisation or nation to form one that is independent.

Sergeant Soldier who is in charge of a company.

Shrapnel Fragments from an exploded artillery shell, mine, or bomb.

Siege Surrounding an army and waiting for them to surrender.

Uniform Clothing that soldiers wear that are the same for everyone.

Important battles of the American Civil War

The Battle of First Manassas
21st July, 1861

**The Battle of Hampton Roads
(CSS *Merrimack* vs. USS *Monitor*)**
9th March, 1862

The Seven Days
26th June – 2nd July, 1862

The Battle of Sharpsburg
17th September, 1862

The Siege of Vicksburg
18th May – 4th July, 1863

The Battle of Gettysburg
1st – 3rd July, 1863

The Siege of Petersburg
15th June, 1864 – 2nd April, 1865

Index